# John Flavel

## A Famous Dartmouth Puritan

by

**RAY FREEMAN**

**Dartmouth History Research Group**

**ISBN 1 899011 20 X**

# LIST OF ILLUSTRATIONS



**Note on the spelling of Flavel/Flavell:** In the 17th century the name was usually spelt with two "ll"s, but the spelling in this booklet follows that used since the early 18th century by his followers.

# JOHN FLAVEL

Who was John Flavel, and why does Dartmouth have a church, a meeting hall and now a proposed new Community Centre named after him?

The story begins at a time of great religious and political upheaval in the 17th century which culminated in the 1640's with a Civil War in which Dartmouth was heavily involved. At the time there was only one legal church, the Church of England, which in fact contained people of widely different beliefs. Everyone was obliged to attend its services, or pay a fine for not doing so, an escape taken only by a few rich Catholic families. Many of the worshippers hoped that the Church would adopt more "puritan" beliefs - a term of contempt used by their opponents. For instance, some, like the Presbyterians in Scotland, wished to allow the parishioners to play a part in who was appointed as their minister, and believed in keeping the Sabbath day strictly as a day for prayer. King Charles and Archbishop Laud favoured the "High Church" policy which gave the king more political power and the bishops control over who became vicars in the churches. Members of Parliament were struggling to prevent the King ruling without Parliament at all, as he had done for 11 years before 1640 until shortage of money had forced him to summon them to Westminster. Although there were innumerable shades of opinion on politics and religion, it was broadly true that those who wished to limit the powers of the King and compel him to rule through Parliament tended to be Puritan, while those who were willing to allow the King absolute power belonged to the High Church party. Religious and political beliefs affected every person in the land, and the struggles about them in this century established many of the liberties which we hold dear today.

The Corporation of Dartmouth - equivalent to our Town Council - in 1640 was dominated by merchants who feared the King wished to increase his power. The Corporation in those days selected the two M.P.s to represent the town and chose Roger Mathews and Samuel Browne who both supported John Pym, the leader of the opposition to Charles in the House of Commons In 1635, when the old vicar of St. Saviours died, they had used their right as patrons to appoint Anthony Harford, a Puritan, to succeed him. When the Civil War broke out the town, like Exeter and Plymouth, supported Parliament. They armed themselves against an expected Royalist attack in 1643, with every approach road fortified and guns mounted on the tops of both Townstal and St. Saviour's Churches. Prince Maurice, the King's General, captured the town for the Royalists in October 1643 after a month's siege. The Puritan vicar Anthony Harford, fled. Dartmouth was occupied by Royalists for three years and those who had fought for Parliament were imprisoned, their ships, houses and goods seized. By 1646 the Royalists had lost the war elsewhere, and General Fairfax recaptured Dartmouth for Parliament. After a short second round of Civil War Charles was captured, tried and executed in 1649.

For the next eleven years England was ruled under a Protectorate headed by Oliver Cromwell, a leading Puritan. Clergy who opposed Puritan beliefs were expelled from their livings, as happened in Stoke Fleming and Dittisham. Anthony Harford, who had fled from Dartmouth when it fell to the Royalists, returned in 1646 and served as vicar until his death in 1654.

## 1656 JOHN FLAVEL ARRIVES IN DARTMOUTH.

There was then a dispute over who should succeed Harford. Thomas Boone, the rich owner of Mount Boone House and a close friend of Cromwell, favoured John Flavel, a young man reputed to be a fine preacher. He had been born in 1630 at Bromsgrove, Worcestershire, the elder son of the Rev. Richard Flavel who brought him up to share his own Presbyterian beliefs. He went up to University College Oxford where he studied for two years. In 1650 he was appointed assistant to the rector of Diptford, who was then old and ill, and succeeded him on the latter's death. The town Corporation, led by William Barnes and Joseph Cubitt, who had for many years had the right to choose the vicar, preferred Allen Geare. In 1656 it was decided that both men should be appointed, Flavel to St. Clements at Townstal and Geare to St. Saviours, and the two men worked amicably together for the short time left of rule by the Protectorate. James Burdwood was the minister at St. Petrox church at this time. After Cromwell's death Charles II returned as king in 1660.

Now all those who had supported Cromwell were punished by a series of laws passed by the High Church parliament. Two thousand clergy who refused to accept the Church of England Prayer Book, including Geare, Burdwood and Flavel, were ejected from their livings in 1662, and Geare died shortly afterwards.

Before the Civil War it had been hoped that all shades of opinion could worship together in one church. After the war it was evident that this was impossible as so many different beliefs had been allowed to grow under Cromwell. Now all who refused to conform to the Church of England with its bishops, prayer book and Thirty Nine Articles, were barred from Parliament, universities, town councils and from taking any part in public life. The entire Dartmouth Corporation

*1. An oil painting of John Flavel.*

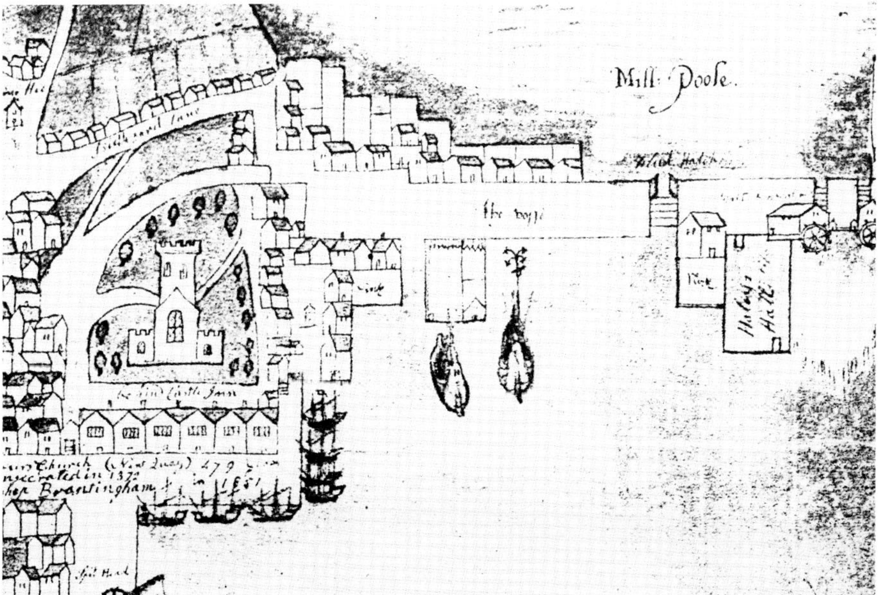


*2. St. Saviour's Church, where John Flavel was Vicar from 1656-62, as depicted in a 17th century drawing*

3. *Doric columns in Fosse Street which led to the first meeting place of Flavel's followers.*

4. *The Flavel Church as enlarged in 1841, seen in a 19th century photograph.*

had to resign. Dissenters (also called non-conformists) ranging from Catholics to numerous different sorts of former Puritans were all forbidden to hold their own services even secretly in their own houses and were fined 12 pence for not attending the Church of England.

## FLAVEL'S LIFE AS A SECRET PASTOR

John Flavel was to play a leading part in the story of Dartmouth over the next thirty years even though he was no longer vicar. Both he and James Burdwood are listed in 1665 as non-conformists who held private meetings. Their followers believed that they were entitled to choose their ministers for themselves. Those fined for not attending the church of England included families like Plumleigh and Taylor who had been leading citizens for many years. Flavel's parents were also suffering for their beliefs. In 1665 they had been arrested for holding illegal services under the new laws and thrown into Newgate Prison, London: both died of the plague they contracted there.

After he had been ejected as vicar, John Flavel tried to earn a living by setting up a small school, or academy, for Dissenters in Dartmouth. However, under the new Five Mile Act, ejected ministers were forbidden to teach in schools within 5 miles of a chartered town - as Dartmouth was - so he was forced to move to Slapton. Not being allowed by the new laws to preach, he held services secretly in woods, or slipped back into Dartmouth to meet followers in private houses. At all times he was liable to be arrested and his life must have been like that of secret agents in war-time France under Nazi occupation. He once rode to Totnes disguised as a woman to baptise a baby. He sometimes held meetings on the Saltstone, in the middle of Salcombe estuary, which was accessible only at low water at Spring tides. When pursued by those out to arrest him he once escaped by riding his horse into the sea and swimming it round to Slapton Sands. For a time he was sheltered and supported by the Rolle family at Hudscott Hall near South Molton, Devon, where he enjoyed beautiful gardens and plantations which inspired him to write a book, *Husbandry Spiritualised*.

In 1672 Charles II, hoping to help Catholics with whom he sympathised, passed a Declaration of Indulgence by which Flavel was allowed to return to Dartmouth as a licensed preacher. It is thought that Flavel's followers then began to meet in a small room on the site of part of the present Flavel Hall, approached through an arch from Foss St. However, this Indulgence was soon withdrawn, and Flavel decided to leave by ship for London. The ship was caught in a great tempest. Flavel prayed and committed the ship's company to God in expectation that they would soon be wrecked on Portland Bill. Suddenly, as if in answer to prayer, the wind changed and they were saved. During the next few years, while living in London, Flavel wrote many sermons and books, hoping to continue his ministry in print since he was prevented by the laws from preaching publicly. Three, *The Seaman's Companion*, *Sea Deliverances* and *Navigation Spiritualised*, reflected his concerns for seamen after his ordeal on the ship.His many publications were widely read for over a century.

In 1684 Flavel returned to Dartmouth and preached to his supporters. He was soon placed under house arrest, and his enemies burned his effigy on a bonfire. In 1687 the next king, the Catholic James II, announced a policy of religious toleration and Flavel was able to preach openly again.

By this time his name was known outside his immediate community among other dissenting groups, and it was clear that it would be of benefit for the smaller of these to combine. In 1691 he travelled to Topsham, preaching what proved to be his last sermon at Ashburton, to preside as Moderator of a meeting of non-conformist ministers of Devonshire at Topsham. He urged that those calling themselves Presbyterians and Congregationalists should combine, as they had done in London. He secured a unanimous agreement to this union, which set up the Exeter Assembly to preside over non-conformist affairs in Devon and Cornwall and lasted until 1753.

Almost immediately afterwards, at supper that evening, Flavel suffered a stroke and died. His body was carried back to Dartmouth, accompanied by growing numbers of mourners all the way. He was buried near the Chancel in St. Saviour's - a traditional right for all former vicars - and a memorial tablet was placed nearby.

"Could Grace or Learning from the Grave set free
Flavel thou hadst not seen Mortality.
Tho' here thy Dusty Part Death's victim lies
Thou by thy Works thyself dost Eternize,
Which Death nor Rust of time shall overthrow:
Whilst thou dost reign above, these live below."

In 1709 the Magistrates of Dartmouth Corporation ordered its removal from St. Saviour's, and it was then placed in the meeting hall behind Foss St. which had become the Independent Chapel.

## FLAVEL'S CHURCH AFTER HIS DEATH.

After 1689 when William III became king non-conformists were no longer actively persecuted, though they were still excluded from parliament, all public offices and the universities. Flavel's followers continued to worship in the small building behind Foss Street, which in 1735 acquired a Communion Plate inscribed "Presbyterian Chapel". It was by this name they were then known, and records show that there were 450 Presbyterians living in the town at this time.

In the late 17th and 18th centuries many French Huguenots, whose religious views were very similar, settled in Dartmouth and formed their own church. One of their pastors, Rev. André Majendie, was assistant at the Flavel chapel. In 1784 the building was again enlarged, and it may be from this time that a pair of Doric columns were erected in Foss St. to mark the entrance to the chapel behind. They can be seen in late 19th century photographs.

In 1810 the Rev. Thomas Stenner arrived as minister, the start of a truly remarkable family ministry which lasted under Thomas until 1849 and continued under the Rev. John Flavel Stenner from 1850-1861. It was during this time in 1811 that the General and Independent Sunday School was started, the first in the district. It should be remembered that, in the days when no public provision was made for educating the poor, the Sunday Schools were the first to provide a chance for such children to learn to read and write. In 1832 the church was affiliated to the Congregational Union. Between 1831 and 1841 new churches were formed at Galmpton, Dittisham and Stoke Fleming.

In 1841 the Rev. Thomas Stenner acquired additional land for a much enlarged meeting house. It was described as "a very handsome building, with two tiers of galleries on the north, south and west sides and a single gallery behind the pulpit on the east side." There was a tower on the northeast corner.

From 1876-1909 the minister was the Rev. John Thomas Ham Paynter, a most active worker. Church buildings were open for activities every night of the week, and he was known nationally as well as locally. He was for many years the Chairman of the Local Education Committee.

A map of 1891 shows the Congregational chapel as having seating for 650 and there was a tower on the north east corner that was 18 inches higher than St. Saviour's church. During the 19th and early 20th centuries the numbers of people worshipping at the Chapel remained high, and there was a considerable social life organised around it for members. The Sunday School grew so fast that it was too small for its numbers.

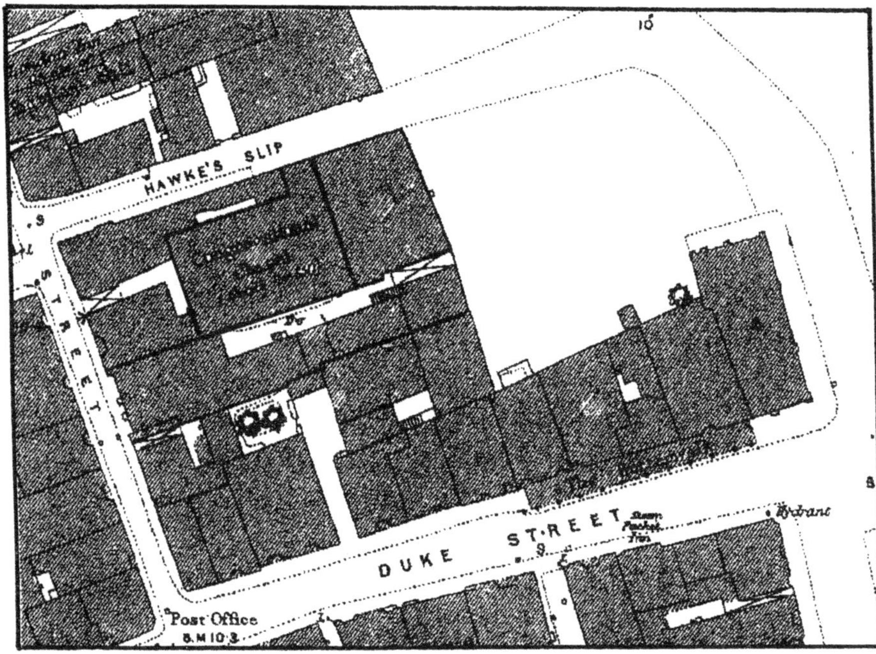


*5. A map of 1891 shows the Congregational Chapel off Hawke's Slip.*

In 1878 the Town Council began a major land reclamation scheme in which the area known as the Mill Pool, between Foss Street and the New Ground, was reclaimed from the sea. The Flavel Trustees saw the opportunity for acquiring a site for a new building,. At first they thought this would be for a Sunday School, but in the end decided to build a new church and use the old building as the Sunday School. In 1895 they began building the present Flavel Church which opened in 1896.

The old church was completely changed providing not only a Sunday School but a Lecture Room holding 120 people, and a Hall for concerts and public

6. *Site of the new Flavel Church just being reclaimed from the old Pool in 1891.*

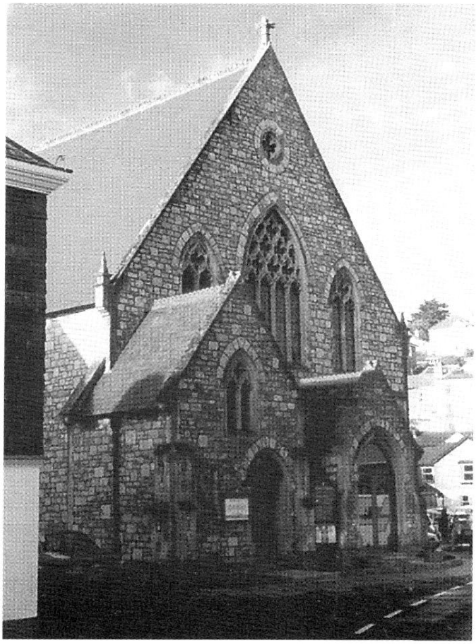

7. *The Flavel Church completed. It opened in 1896.*

8. *The Flavel Sunday School after bomb damage in February 1943. This was replaced by the Flavel Hall in 1954.*

9. *An artist's impression of the new Flavel Centre, on the site of the Flavel Hall.*

meetings. On the death of the Rev. Paynter in 1909 the Church had 200 members, the Sunday School had 300 children with 40 teachers, and the choir of 40 provided high quality music.

Between 1909 - 1918 the church prospered, and Mrs Elliot. the Minister's wife, started the Women's Meeting. During the First World War the church lost several of its young men, including the sons of the Minister and of the Church Treasurerer.

Between the two wars the church continued to flourish, particularly under Rev. W. Zeal, when membership equalled that under the Rev. Paynter. However, the building of a large Council estate up at Townstal which started in 1937 took many children away from the town centre and drastically affected the Sunday School.

In 1939 at the outbreak of the Second World War the Borough Council commandeered the Sunday School at a very low rent. All weekday activities were forced to cease. Even worse was to follow in February 1943 when a German bombing raid hit Duke Street and the Sunday School was damaged beyond repair. The Church too was seriously damaged, and out of action for three years.

After the war, under the Rev. Ernest Smith, the present Flavel Hall was built on the site of the Sunday School. The amount of compensation received for war damage was quite inadequate, and the Church raised thousands of pounds towards its cost. It was opened in 1954, and soon proved its usefulness not only to the Church but to the town as a meeting place for many societies as well as acting as a theatre for amateur dramatics.

Up to 1969 the Church had its own Minister, but since then it has shared its Minister first with Totnes and then with Brixham. In 1974 the Flavel Memorial Congregational Church became the United Reformed Church. In 1985 they were joined by the Methodists and became the Methodist and United Reformed Church.

THE PROPOSED NEW FLAVEL COMMUNITY CENTRE.

When Devon County Council began looking for a site for a larger library for Dartmouth in the town centre, the Trustees of the Flavel Church were discussing the future of their Hall. It was suggested that its site could be combined with the adjoining former Fire Station for a fine new building for the town. The idea was taken up by the Dartmouth and Kingswear Society, who put forward a scheme for a combined Library and Community Centre, using this site for a variety of activities for which premises were sorely needed. As it would be on the site where John Flavel's followers first met over three hundred years ago, the project was called after him, the Flavel Community Centre. The Flavel Church Trustees propose to sell their Hall and with the money provide rooms for their purposes in the Church. With promises of money from South Hams District Council, Dartmouth Town Council, Devon County Council and much local fundraising, it is hoped to get other funding from public agencies and grant giving trusts.

The new Community Centre is designed to provide the following facilities:

* It will comply with the Disabled Disabilities Act 1996, with easy access to the ground floor and lifts to other floors.

* There will be a modern multi-media library and life-long learning centre on the ground floor and an Information Technology suite with full internet access to encourage people of all ages to develop computer skills.

* For drama productions and films there will be a multi-purpose Community Hall with retractable raked seating for 200, high quality accoustics, a stage, theatre lighting, and full projection facilities.

* Catering facilities will be available for meetings and functions.

* Meeting rooms will cater for a wide variety of public and private activities.

* A foyer café on the ground floor will have a drop-in facility for library users, residents and visitors.

## ACKNOWLEDGEMENTS.

This paper is based on information in the following publications:

Edward Windeatt: John Flavell, a Notable Dartmouth Puritan, Transactions of the Devonshire Association, 1911.

Percy Russell: Flavel Memorial United Reformed Church, Dartmouth, 1974.

Flavel Church: Highlights of the History of the Flavel Church.

James Kelly: Flavell, John, alias Flavel, entry in New Dictionary of National Biography. 2001.

Unknown Life of John Flavel, pub. by the Ages Digital Library. 1997.

Ray Freeman: Dartmouth and its Neighbours, Dartbooks 1997.

Flavel Centre Trust: The Flavel Centre - Brochure on the current proposals, 2001.

Photographs: The Dartmouth Museum , The Flavel Church Trustees and Harold Hutchins.

## Previous Publications by the Dartmouth History Research Group.

1. The Holdsworth and Newman Families in Dartmouth. by Ray Freeman
2. Dartmouth Cottage Hospital. A History by Dr. W. G. Keane
3. The Dartmouth Residences of Thomas Newcomen and his Family. by I. H. Smart.
4. Brownstone: A Devon Farm Through Seven Centuries. by Ray Freeman.
5. The Guildhalls of Dartmouth. by I. H. Smart
6. The Free French in Kingswear. by Tony Higgins
7. The Newcomen Memorials in Dartmouth. by I. H. Smart.
8. The Story of Warfleet. by Ray Freeman.
9. Oldstone . The Story of a Ruined Mansion. by Ursula Dimes.
10. Wrecks off the South Devon Coast. by Tony Aylmer.
11. We Remember D-Day. Compiled by Ray Freeman.
12. A Wrens-Eye View of Wartime Dartmouth. Compiled by Ray Freeman.
13. The Development of Dartmouth Millpond. by I. H. Smart.
15. The Newcomen Road . by I. H. Smart
16. Memories of War. Compiled by Ray Freeman
17. River Dart Pilotage. By Dave Griffiths
18. Dartmouth Industry and Banking 1795 to 1925. By I H Smart
19. Sir Thomas Wilton JP CA. A Biography. By Dr T N P N Wilton
20. Operation Fahrenheit. By Michel Guillou
21. Wadstray House. By Irene O'Shea
22. A Dittisham Boy's Story. By Ewart Hutchins
23. The Secret War from the River Dart. By Lloyd Bott
24. Hawley's Fortalice, Dartmouth's First Castle. By Terry Edwards
25. The History of the Castle Hotel, Dartmouth. By Ray Freeman
26. William Veale, Master Mariner, 1791 - 1867. By Linda King
27. The Torbay Paint Company. By Bridget Howard
28. Sportspeople of Dartmouth. By Alan Coles

Available from:

The Dartmouth Museum, The Butterwalk, Dartmouth, Devon. TQ6 9PZ

The Harbour Bookshop, 12 Fairfax Place, Dartmouth, Devon, TQ6 9AE
Tel. and Fax. (0803) 832448. Overseas orders welcome.